DOLLS

Kay Desmonde   Photographs by Angelo Hornak

TREASURE PRESS

First published in Great Britain in 1974 by
Octopus Books Ltd
as *All Colour Book of Dolls*

This edition published in 1984 by
Treasure Press
59 Grosvenor Street
London W1

© 1974 Octopus Books Ltd

ISBN 0 907812 76 7

Printed in Hong Kong

Sets designed by
Laura Cecil & Angelo Hornak

CONTENTS

Introduction

Dolls, dolls and still more dolls.

When thinking of a doll today one immediately brings to mind a small girl's plaything, but if we go back in history we learn that the doll, as we know it, appears only in comparatively recent years. The doll in the form of a human being existed for thousands of years before ever being given to a child as a plaything. At first, small figures in human form had their place as idols for primitive people. The earliest ones would have been made of readily available materials, such as wood or stone, and would have had a natural form suggesting a human figure; perhaps a branch with twigs giving a resemblance to limbs, or a stone bearing some resemblance to a human face or figure which could be easily modified into instantly recognizable features. Primitive people, like children, can easily imagine human form in such things but today we have become so sophisticated that small stone dolls with their head, body and limbs all in one piece would hardly appear to most of us as figures at all — although to their early worshippers they presumably seemed very realistic indeed. The first doll-like figures man modelled in clay possibly present the earliest evidence of intellect among primitive people, for no animal, not even the most intelligent, can create an image of himself.

In pre-Roman times dolls had a magical and mystical significance and were therefore only handled by priests and medicine men. Children would certainly never have been allowed to handle such awe-inspiring objects, which their worshippers believed held the power of life and death. Later, in early Greek and Roman times, children did have dolls as playthings. It is known that little girls made clothes for their dolls and on marrying dedicated them to a deity, usually the Greek goddess Artemis, known to Roman children as Diana. It is possible that the play doll had developed from the early religious figures, which may have been handed on to children after the belief in their magical powers had declined. The doll is often mentioned in Greek and Roman literature and was evidently more commonplace then than during the subsequent period, although the doll did not disappear completely in medieval times. The Latin for a girl baby was *pupa,* from which developed the English word puppet, the German word for doll, which is *Puppe,* and the French word *poupée.*

From the early fifteenth century, dollmakers have been recorded in Nuremberg, but unfortunately very few of their dolls remain, having been made of wood and rags, materials unable to withstand the ravages of time as had the earlier stone dolls. Paintings of the period show little girls playing with dolls dressed as fashionable ladies. The dolls were of course handmade and were comparatively simple, the carved wooden head being attached to a body which may have been either a bundle of rags, or a leather bag filled with bran. Arms and legs were sometimes attached to the body by tapes. Sometimes there were no legs at all, the body finishing at the waist and then fastened to a hoop petticoat over which the doll's dress was sewn.

In the old paintings the doll is often dressed in clothes identical to those of the child holding her. Both outfits would be replicas of an adult costume, for there were no specifically children's fashions; a little girl was dressed as a miniature adult. Most of these dolls would have been especially made for children of wealthy families, but some were made for general sale; in a description of Paris written in the fifteenth century, stalls at the Palais de Justice are described as having charming and attractively dressed dolls for sale.

The French, being a very practical race, used their large dolls to advertise the latest fashions. Before there were newspapers — even before there was any mechanical means of printing — the doll was used to popularize French fashion abroad. From the fourteenth century elaborately outfitted dolls were sent from France to all the courts of Europe, so that royal ladies could have the latest French fashions copied right down to the last detail, including the underwear. Not only were the clothes on the mannequin an exact copy of what the most fashionable French ladies were wearing, the hair was also arranged in the latest styles. So important were these fashion dolls considered to be, both to the sellers and to the buyers, that even wars were not allowed to hinder their despatch and special passes were given to ships carrying them. Such dolls, which were mostly life size although a few were half-life size, were known as 'Pandoras' until the eighteenth century, when they became known as the 'dolls of the Rue St Honoré', the street which was then the centre of the Parisian dressmakers.

Towards the end of the eighteenth century, a new kind of figure for the displaying of fashions was developed in England. This was a sheet of paper with a figure to be cut out printed on it, together with many changes of costume. These were inexpensive, and became very popular. Because of this, and the advent of the fashion magazine, with its many colour plates of the latest styles, the need to send expensive mannequin dolls ceased.

The later French doll, now known as a 'French fashion doll', had nothing to do with the publicizing of French fashions abroad; it was just a beautiful luxury doll. This does not mean that it was not occasionally used for display in shop windows; even today in France one may see miniature shop window models for displaying fashion, and very attractive these tiny modern mannequins are.

Because of its cheapness and availability, wood has always been used for making dolls. There is virtually no documentation of the few dolls remaining from the seventeenth century, so it is very difficult to date these early wooden dolls with accuracy. 'Queen Anne' is the name given to dolls made between 1700 and 1780, although Queen Anne herself only reigned for twelve years from 1702. It seems ironic that her name should be given to a type of doll, for although she bore seventeen children, only one survived infancy — and he, the Duke of Gloucester, died when he was eleven — so it is unlikely that there were many dolls in the royal nursery during her reign. These early wooden dolls, which we can still find occasionally, were made in England

It is believed that tomb dolls originated as a replacement for human sacrifice. From earliest times, in all parts of the world, widows and servants were put to death to accompany a dead man on his journey into the next world. Later, when life was held in higher esteem and this barbaric custom ceased, a substitute had to be found. Egypt has given us the richest treasure trove of tomb dolls. From 1600 BC tomb dolls were produced on a large scale, made of clay, wood or any available local stone, which was often inlaid with pieces of coloured glass. These three dolls came from the estate of a Devon clergyman who was an ardent Egyptologist.

where the guilds were less strict than in other parts of Europe. English wood carvers were able to paint and then to finish off their dolls themselves; on the continent, where the guilds appear to have been as strong as Trades Unions are today, a wood carver was not allowed to paint his doll. It had to be passed to a bismuth painter and then on to someone else to dress and finish.

The earliest of these wooden dolls had eyes carved into the wood and painted, but from about 1700, glass eyes were used. These were black and pupil-less with very little of the white showing, the eyebrows and eyelashes being simulated by small painted dots. Some of the dolls which survive from about 1780 had blue eyes with pupils. The more expensive dolls had long, finely carved fingers on their wooden arms. The cheaper ones had crudely made arms of either cloth or leather.

As the century progressed, and with it the need for a cheaper product to compete with the dolls which were then coming into Britain from other parts of Europe, the quality of the English doll deteriorated. Although wooden dolls were still made in England, more and more were imported from Germany and the peg wooden dolls were known as 'Dutch' dolls. ('Dutch' in this instance is a variant of 'Deutsch' [German] for these dolls were mostly bought through the wholesalers of Nuremberg.) The peg wooden dolls were so-called because of the tiny wooden

pegs which held the articulated limbs in position, whether they were made with ball-and-socket joints or the cruder mortise-and-tenon joints.

By the beginning of the nineteenth century Nuremberg was the toy distributing centre of the world. Dolls were not made there, but were brought in from all the surrounding areas and then distributed. Peg wooden dolls were made from half an inch up to three feet in size, and many survive in their original clothes. An amazing number of the very tiny ones still come to light in almost mint condition, the miniature clothes exquisitely made, the doll often wearing a high bonnet to cover a comb carved at the top of the head.

The quality of the wooden dolls subsequently deteriorated, until by the end of the nineteenth century they became very crude, and have never regained their former quality. They are made in a crude manner even today, in the South Tyrol (now Italian though formerly a part of Austria), where the majority of these dolls were made in the past when their manufacture was at its peak. The painted hair style of these dolls remains the same today as it was in about 1865, unlike the earlier dolls which had followed the hair fashions of the period in which they were made.

Dolls made of wax have been recorded since the seventeenth century and there are wonderful examples of the early wax dolls in museums. They were finely made and beautifully dressed in contemporary clothes. Because of their fragility these dolls (the ones which have survived anyway) must have been kept either in glazed wooden cases or under glass domes all the time, for apart from some fading of both the wax and the dress materials these dolls are in remarkably good condition. The wax used for modelling was mostly beeswax with additives to give durability. The earlier wax heads were made from a solid lump of wax either carved or sculpted into shape. The heads and limbs of the luxury wax dolls of the mid-nineteenth century were made by pouring liquid wax into moulds; consequently they are often called 'poured wax' dolls.

There were many listed wax dollmakers, the two most famous being the Montanari and the Pierotti families, who made dolls in England through several generations. The last Pierotti dollmaker retired in 1935. The wax dolls made by these two families were very attractive and lifelike. They were beautifully modelled and had glass eyes, and the hair, and often eyebrows and eyelashes as well, was inserted into the wax in a very realistic manner. They were expensive dolls, some undressed ones selling at five guineas, which was a very high price for a child's toy in Victorian times, so they must have been the treasured possessions only of children of wealthy parents. Madame Augusta Montanari made and marketed the first real baby dolls. Prior to this the dolls' bodies were always in adult form with narrow waists to take the fashions of the day. At the Great Exhibition held in Hyde Park in London in 1851 Madame Montanari won a prize for her wax dolls which portrayed all ages from infancy to adulthood. The wax baby dolls which we are fortunately still able to find today are usually dressed in beautiful hand-stitched baby clothes, even the smallest garment, the flannel binder, being bound in pure silk with the minutest of stitches. Some of the dresses have matching petticoats and are works of art with their narrow tucking and lace insertion. The hours and hours of work put into the making of a doll's trousseau make one realize the different tempo of life then compared with that of today.

A cheaper type of wax doll sold in the nineteenth century was made of papier mâché, or other forms of composition material, which was moulded and painted and then dipped in wax. These dolls had either a wig glued on or hair inserted in a slit at the top of their heads, with the hair arranged smoothly from the centre parting and falling in ringlets over the ears. Wax-over-composition dolls are not so durable as poured wax ones since the differing expansion and contraction rates of the wax and the composition underneath made these heads very susceptible to cracking. The earlier dolls of this type are often spurned because of their crazed faces, which some people think detracts from their charm; personally I find them very endearing.

Papier mâché heads for dolls were made from the sixteenth century onwards, mostly in France, but from 1810 the German toy factories at Sonneberg mass-produced these heads in moulds, using a pressure process which eliminated the kneading together by hand of the ingredients, which were paper, glue and sand. Such heads became very popular and were attached either to an all-cloth stuffed body with leather arms or to a fine leather body with wooden half arms and legs. Their moulded hair styles closely followed the fashion of the day and these dolls are more easily dated than probably any other type, for the hair fashions were very short lived. These papier mâché dolls' heads continued to be popular until about 1860.

At the same time as the papier mâché dolls were enjoying popularity, china and bisque heads for dolls were also being made. Their fashionable hair styles were moulded in the porcelain, and some also had moulded bonnets, hats and flowers, ribbons and feathers. Two types of porcelain were used, the glazed hard-paste porcelain known as 'china' and the unglazed porcelain known as 'bisque'. Some of the early untinted bisque dolls are now called 'parian' by collectors.

The glazed porcelain was the more popular in the first half of the nineteenth century and some of the famous porcelain factories, such as Dresden and Copenhagen, made dolls' heads of superb quality. The unglazed porcelain heads were more delicately coloured, and it is among these that one finds more decoration — bonnets with feather or flower decoration, snoods and ribbons. Heads, arms and legs, as well as complete dolls, were sold, so that one could buy the parts and put together one's own doll at home. These heads were incorporated with shoulder plates to be glued to the cloth body, or sewn, in the case of those with eyelet holes.

A swivel socket neck, patented in France by Mme Huret in 1861, began a new era in doll manufacture, for the doll was no longer limited to staring stiffly to the front; the head could now be turned from side to side. These heads were still models of adult ladies and were usually attached to rigid leather bodies, but a few of the later fashion-type heads used the newer patented spring-jointed bodies, which gave movement to the limbs as well. Painted-on hair was replaced by wigs made of materials giving a more realistic appearance: flax, silk, mohair (hair from the Angora goat), and sometimes even human hair was used. These beautiful bisque-headed dolls made in France are possibly the most exquisite play dolls ever produced. These are the dolls that are today sometimes called 'fashion dolls' for the dolls were dressed in the style of clothes fashionable at the time. There were shops in Paris which sold only dolls' clothes and accessories, all reflecting the latest in adult fashion complete to the last detail. Besides hats, shoes and jewelry, accessories included powder boxes, miniature books, rosaries, lorgnettes, opera glasses, brushes, combs and mirrors. For a doll dressed as a bride, there was even a complete dinner service with cutlery fitted into a small trunk.

From the late 1870s the wood-and-composition ball-and-socket jointed body was used for a new type of doll: one with such flexible limbs that it could sit down. This was the start of what is known as the golden era in the manufacture of dolls. The doll now looked more like a young girl and as there were no baby dolls with rounded limbs — these came much later — the little girl doll was often dressed as a new-born baby with a complete layette of hand-stitched baby clothes. The Victorian child could quite happily imagine that she was playing with a new-born baby. Kid bodies were still made, but they were gradually superseded by the ball-and-socket jointed bodies.

Mass production increased and doll factories in France were now turning out millions of dolls annually. Painted eyes had by now been almost completely replaced by realistic glass ones. Dolls now had movement, some walked, crawled, swam and talked and every year there was some new invention that made the doll more lifelike. Superlative dolls made by the most famous French doll manufacturers, such as Jumeau, Bru, Gesland, and Steiner, won medals at exhibitions all over the world.

Meanwhile, Germany was rebuilding her doll industry and was soon supplying china heads to many countries at about a quarter of the price for which the French could sell them. Over a period of years this gradually ruined the French doll industry, so that by 1899 the major French doll companies had to amalgamate to try and ward off complete financial disaster. Germany's dominance continued to increase and German dollmakers brought out many different types of doll, real baby dolls with bald heads, dolls with heads modelled on real children known as 'character heads', coloured dolls etc. Most of them had bisque heads, but a new material was also being

used: celluloid. This was first made in the mid-nineteenth
century in England from camphor, which gave it its characteristic
odour, and cellulose nitrate, which is explosive gun-cotton used
for blasting. This was a dangerous material for children's toys,
as it was highly inflammable, but it was light in weight,
washable, and cheaper than bisque, so it had some success. At

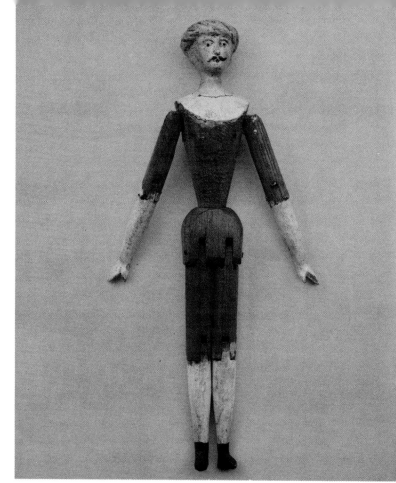

Right
This is an unusual head to find on a peg wooden body.
A male doll is always a rare collectors' item but this one
dating from 1840 is exceptionally fine; the mortise-and-
tenon jointing can be seen clearly. The features, including
the moustache, are painted and the hat is not carved but
appears to have been moulded from some kind of plaster
and then painted in one with the head. The painting of
these dolls is interesting, for water colours were used and
then a clear varnish was applied giving a translucent effect;
the later dolls were painted with enamel paint.

Below
A doll of the Pierotti type dressed as a bride, with two
small wax-over-composition pages. After 1860 wedding
veils covered the bride's face, so this doll with its veil held
away from the face by sprigs of orange blossom, was
possibly dressed about 1855. The off-the-shoulder gown
is probably a copy of the wedding dress of the original
owner. The later page boys, made around 1875, are
beautifully dressed in velvet trimmed with handmade lace,
and as they are in mint condition one assumes they were
also dressed in copies of suits worn for a special occasion,
and then put away and kept as a memento.

first, celluloid heads were used on the jointed wood-and-composition bodies and on kid bodies, and were made in moulds identical to those used for bisque heads; later both heads and bodies were made of celluloid, and these continued to be produced until the 1930s.

Germany led the world in dollmaking until the onset of World War I, when she lost some of her major markets such as Britain and later the United States. As imports of dolls from Germany ceased on the outbreak of war, the British had to turn elsewhere for dolls and toys to stock the toyshops. (Despite being the makers of superb porcelain, the British themselves never made dolls' heads of the quality achieved by the French and German factories.) Britain's major source of supply during the war years was Japan, who was then an ally. Japan copied successfully the popular types of doll heads – too successfully at first, for Japanese-made dolls arrived in Britain with the 'made in Germany' also copied.

Rag dolls also had their place in the doll world during this period. In earlier times they were not as common as wooden or clay dolls, as cloth was a valuable material and would not have been used to make a child's toy, but from Victorian times rag dolls were made, mostly at home. In the late nineteenth century sheets of linen were sold printed with a doll figure to be cut out and sewn together; sometimes they had complete outfits as well. Made up at home, these dolls were inexpensive, and sold very well, continuing to be popular right through World War I, when other dolls were more difficult to obtain. Dean's Rag Book Company secured many patents for different types of rag doll. Unfortunately most of the early rag dolls have disappeared as they are subject to attack by moths and mice.

When thinking of rag dolls, that is dolls made from textiles, one must not forget the stockinet dolls made in the United States of America by Martha Chase from the 1880s or the very naturalistic child dolls made by Kathe Kruse in Germany from 1910 on. In the 1920s and 1930s the most popular rag dolls in England were those made by Norah Wellings and Chad Valley; and there were the Lenci dolls made in Italy by Enrico Scavini. ('Lenci' was Scavini's pet name for his wife.) All these dolls enjoyed a wide popularity as their predecessors had been so fragile. Although all the leading doll manufacturers had experimented with different materials in an effort to produce a truly unbreakable doll, the only ones which really lived up to the name 'unbreakable' were of cloth or rubber. Rubber dolls had been made since the mid-nineteenth century when Charles Goodyear discovered a method of vulcanizing rubber so that it would hold its shape, but few of these hard rubber dolls have survived. In the 1920s softer rubber baby dolls were made and these were very successful.

After World War I Germany came back into prominence with dolls similar to the ones made before 1914 – although they never achieved the quality of those made in the late Victorian period. Some of the dolls' heads were not fired, the colour being simply painted on the bisque, and so the child could not wash the doll without removing the paint. Towards the end of the 1920s, still using similar moulds to the earlier bisque heads, a new composition material was introduced, the main ingredients being flour and gum. These dolls were highly coloured and lacked the delicacy of the earlier ones.

Since 1945 another new material has been used in dollmaking, and this time it appears to have all the qualities that had eluded the earlier manufacturers, being unbreakable, washable, and light in weight. It is plastic. The type used at first was unyielding and hard, but after vinyl was developed a doll could be made which had all these desirable qualities and was soft to the touch as well. Furthermore the manufacture of dolls in this new material was relatively cheap.

For the purpose of this book I have thought of dolls as typifying only play dolls, and have therefore not included all the other variations such as costume dolls and mascot dolls, or the gollywog and the teddy bear.

The word 'doll' is of comparatively recent usage. It is only since the end of the seventeenth century that the word doll has been used to mean a plaything in human likeness. The derivation of the word 'doll' is unknown but it could have been the name given to a gaily dressed toy figure by a pedlar who was shouting his wares at a fair. ('Doll' is a diminutive of Dorothy so it is not difficult to imagine a pedlar who had named a toy figure 'Dorothy' calling out 'Who'll buy my Doll?') In earlier times, when there were no shops as we know them today and country people were served by itinerant pedlars, fairs were held to enable traders to congregate in one place to sell their goods. The fairs were looked forward to with great excitement; people came from many miles around to feast their eyes on the colourful displays, and to enjoy the music and entertainment too. The whole family would go to the fair together and one can imagine how the stalls with gaily coloured toys and baubles would have attracted them, especially the children. The annual fair held in London on St Bartholomew's Day, August 24, starting in the twelfth century, was of great interest. All kinds of goods were sold there and the little toy figures sold by traders were known as 'Bartholomew Babies' before the word doll came into general usage.

From the early years of Queen Victoria's reign, children were encouraged to play with dolls and toys, as the educational value of the doll began to be recognized. Children learn in their play, just as young animals are learning the rudiments of stalking, hunting and so on as they play. A doll in the form of an adult woman and dressed in fashionable clothes would not so easily arouse the maternal instincts in a little girl. A poor child who could not afford a fashionable lady doll would probably be at an advantage, since its substitute for a baby, be it a block of wood or any object easily available which could be wrapped in a cloth, would be given life by its childish imagination. A child does not, of course, need a naturalistic doll, and an indication of likeness can be sufficient. From my childhood in South Yorkshire during the Depression, I can remember my emotion on seeing a small girl of a poor family singing a lullaby to her 'baby doll', actually an empty bottle wrapped in a cloth.

The more sophisticated a society becomes, the more sophisticated will be its manufactured dolls. Today we have dolls which leave little to the imagination anatomically, and which can do practically everything – cry, walk, talk, sing, pray, etc. – and they are within the range of the pockets of most parents, unlike novelty dolls of the late nineteenth century.

Collectors of dolls begin their collections for a variety of reasons. A doll may be seen by chance which reminds one of a long-remembered treasure of one's childhood. Some collectors admire the beauty and workmanship of the dolls. Many older collectors may only feel the need to acquire one or two to make up for not having been able to afford a doll in childhood. A really avid collector feels that she should buy as many dolls as

Left

An all-celluloid baby made in France in 1920 by Petitcollin. The trade mark on the back of the head is an eagle's head. This attractive baby doll with moulded hair and glass eyes was very popular with younger children for it was much lighter in weight than the bisque-headed, wooden-bodied dolls, and it was unbreakable, or virtually so. It could be dented, and if dropped there was a chance it would not break, whereas the bisque heads shattered into hundreds of pieces. Another advantage was that they could be bathed. They were also very much cheaper to produce.

Right

To an ardent collector, it sometimes seems that the complete cataloguing of all the different types and makes of doll will never be completed, for each week one finds a doll either with a mark never seen before or with some variation in the mode of manufacture. This is a recent acquisition, still in her original box. The interesting thing about her is that apart from the usual jointing, she has jointed ankles. She is obviously one of a range of dolls made either by Armand Marseille or his brother-in-law Ernst Heubach, for it has the horseshoe trademark used by both these companies.

possible so as to preserve them, not only by her care, but also by preventing them from going to someone who, in her opinion, would not treat them with the reverence they merit. Some collectors are lonely people who feel that caring for a doll is a substitute for the love of a child. A child will often turn to its doll more during periods of distress than during happier times — and yet a doll seems to symbolize happiness for us all. Dolls are very personal possessions and the only advice to anyone wishing to start a collection is to buy only what gives them pleasure. Fashions in dolls have always been changeable; the most collected dolls today are the late-nineteenth-century bisque-headed dolls. Wax dolls are gaining in popularity too, and in the future it may be the fashion only to collect these.

New collectors should visit museums, read books and then decide what kind of doll they prefer and start from there.

I have endeavoured through the small compass of this book to work through some of the obtainable dolls in date order — each era having its beauty and attraction — right through to the present day. After seeing so many dolls from earlier times, modern plastic dolls may appear to be characterless, but to see a wide-eyed child in a toy shop choosing her new doll makes one realize that today's dolls have their own appeal. They may not be cherished in the same way that the Victorian doll was for she was most likely the only toy a child had. It is hardly the fault of today's child that she has an abundance of everything and so is not able, by the sheer pressure of today's way of life, to lavish the affection that the Victorian child did on her sole toy. We should not dismiss today's doll as characterless but should include a few of the better examples in a comprehensive collection, for plastic may be superseded by some other material and these plastic dolls will become the collector's items of the future.

Some doll collectors today call themselves plangonologists from the classical Greek word 'plangon' which means doll. As more and more people become interested in collecting dolls more regional clubs are being formed, and these local clubs enable members to meet people with similar interests in their own area, to exchange views and to see new acquisitions.

There are many rewarding and fascinating facets to collecting apart from the acquisition of the dolls themselves. One learns something of the countries where the dolls were produced; the differing fashions of clothes and hair through the ages; the types of material used and the colours that were fashionable in different years. One also looks at contemporary paintings and book illustrations with added pleasure. Even those who did not play with dolls as children, and so have no childhood memories of them, can look at dolls right through the ages and enjoy them for their historical value and for the beauty and ingenuity of their workmanship. I hope as you continue through this book that you will find some dolls which will give you pleasure, and which will be of interest; and if any do evoke memories of childhood days, that the memories will be only happy ones.

Early Dolls

WOODEN DOLLS

Below
Three dolls which were bought in 1830 and whose original clothes are still in

remarkably fine condition. The smallest doll is only one and a quarter inches tall but the clothes are beautifully styled. The one on the right with the high carved comb is the type that Queen Victoria dressed when a girl with the help of her governess. These little peg wooden dolls are jointed at the shoulder, elbow, hips and knees and they have tiny carved and painted feet. They were mass-produced in the Grodner Tal district of Austria but similar dolls were also made in England, where a whole family would be concerned with the manufacture – the carving, painting and dressing of the doll all being done at home.

Right
One of the oldest dolls that might be found by a collector today, this fine English wooden doll is known as a 'Queen Anne' type (although she was not made until about 1760 and Queen Anne had died in 1714). The head and body are in one piece, the arms are of leather and the wooden legs are jointed at the hip and knee. The carved head was first covered in gesso and then painted. The black pupil-less glass eyes are a feature of this type of doll – previously eyes had been carved and painted. Unfortunately this particular doll has lost her original clothes.

WOODEN DOLLS

Left

An unusual doll made about 1830. This is the ordinary wooden doll of the period, its features delicately painted, but the whole head and shoulders waxed. The very smooth hairstyle held in place at the back with a brown ribbon also appears to have been lightly waxed, as have the green earrings. The wooden dolls of this period were of good quality, but this one is exceptionally fine and bears no comparison with the crude wooden dolls made later in the century, when the heads were not well shaped — and were as wide as the shoulder — the features poorly painted, and the dolls' hands and feet were just notches in the wood.

Right

Only one of these peg wooden dolls is a genuine Victorian doll, all the others having been made in recent years, three of them exact copies of the earlier dolls. The old doll is the one on the right at the top. Directly under it is a beautifully finished wooden doll, which has no pretensions to Victorian ancestry, made by Dryad. Peg wooden dolls made after 1860 are difficult to date as the mid-19th-century hairstyle appears on all of them right up to the present day. These dolls have always been popular, for they were easy for a child to hold, and they could be simply and effectively dressed by a child learning to sew.

Left

Two wooden shoulder heads from the second half of the 19th century which were sold for attaching to a home-made cloth body. The heads are made of pine and have painted features, the one on the left having a carved hairstyle, while that on the right has a painted domed head with no recognizable hairstyle. These dolls should have made ideal toys with their unbreakable heads, and the soft bodies which a child prefers, but they were not as popular as the peg wooden dolls — possibly because unless the body was tailored and tightly stuffed it would, of course, have been no use for dressing in fashionable clothes.

PAPIER MÂCHÉ DOLLS

Above

This doll standing beside her hand-painted sedan chair has a secret under her skirt: she is mounted on a wide wooden reel, and when placed on a slightly inclined board she appears to walk down it. The hairstyle dates this doll at about 1865 with its puffs and braids at the side and a painted comb holding the smooth chignon at the back. Round her neck is painted a choker necklace and she has painted earrings. This is one of the unusual dolls which occasionally come to light, and make doll collecting such a fascinating hobby.

Right

Papier mâché doll of about 1840 with a hand-sewn fine kid body and wooden lower arms and legs with flat painted feet, known to some collectors as a 'milliner's model'. This doll was sold to me recently by an elderly lady who said that it had been used in her family since her great-grandmother's day as a model on which to design clothes for the daughters of the family. Because of its history, this doll came without its original clothes. This is unusual as these dolls are usually found with all their beautifully fashioned original clothes.

Left

An interesting papier mâché head on its original body made of loosely stuffed linen with leather arms. The body is badly proportioned, which would not have been conducive to the fashioning of fine clothes for her. This may account for these dolls often being found with rather shapeless original clothes. The hair with its long side ringlets and braided bun at the back was the style of 1835, and the material for the clothes is of the same period, so this doll is easily dated.

Wax Dolls

Below
Wax dolls have a beauty all their own, the texture of the material giving such a realistic appearance. This baby doll with its tiny rosebud mouth and blue glass eyes has hair inserted directly into the wax head and hair eyelashes in the moulded eyelids. These dolls are more durable than they at first appear, and to allay fears some makers stamped on the cloth bodies the words 'warranted to stand any climate'. This may have been for the benefit of children being taken to the hotter parts of the British Empire who wished to take their dolls with them.

Opposite above left
A label attached to this wax-over-composition sailor boy doll reads 'One of two dolls (the other was given to Lady Mary Liddell when she was a little girl) which were presented to General Sir G. Walker's children (Anna and Harriet) by the daughters of George III'. No indication is given as to which of the six princesses gave the dolls or why; perhaps it was a combined present from all of them! This doll was diplayed in a museum and dated 1780, but I doubt if it was made before 1800.

Opposite above right
So few wax dolls are marked with the maker's name that it is almost impossible accurately to attribute any one doll to a specific maker. This girl doll, made about 1865, is a Montanari type, finely modelled, with wax limbs attached to the cloth body by sewing through eyelet holes. Madame Augusta Montanari had been making these dolls commercially since about 1850.

Opposite below
This poured wax doll, dating from about 1800, arrived with a cotton pinafore covering her clothes. When this was removed her dress was in immaculate condition underneath, and all the clothes are handsewn with the tiniest of stitches. Her hair is now very sparse, but it had obviously been arranged in a very smooth severe hairstyle by placing single strands of hair directly on to the bald wax head, which would have been a most laborious task. She has tiny pupil-less glass eyes and her wax limbs are glued to her stuffed linen body.

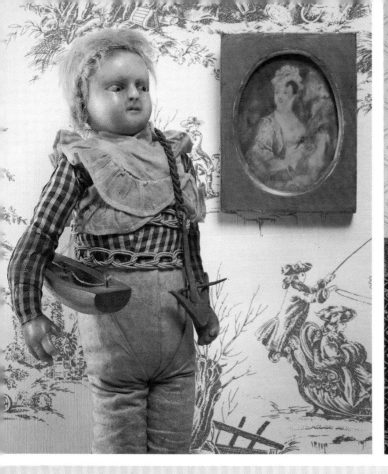

WAX DOLLS

Above

A Regency cradle, with its original chintz covering, containing a later wax-over-composition doll. This was made in Germany by Motschmann after he had seen Japanese dolls at the Paris Exhibition of 1855, which inspired him to make dolls with similar jointing. The head is mounted on a cloth middle torso containing a squeak box, with a composition pelvic section, cloth upper arms and legs, the wooden lower arms having jointed wrists and the wooden lower legs having jointed ankles. This was quite a new type of doll for the European market, for apart from the unusual jointing it also had sleeping eyes operated by a lead weight.

Right

Although not of the finest quality these wax-over-composition dolls were very popular as they were cheap. At one time, they were given away with coupons from Mazawattee tea packets in England, so many children were able to have one. The whole head including the hair is moulded in composition, dipped in wax and then painted. The arms and legs are always of painted wood, with scoop-like hands and flat feet. Such dolls were not very durable and are often seen in very poor condition, but these two are in such a remarkable state of preservation it is difficult to believe that they are over 100 years old.

WAX DOLLS

Above

An amusing Easter gift for a little girl about 1880. The head and limbs are of poured wax and the eggshell is most realistically made of papier mâché. As the head lifts off, it is possible that this was originally a sweet container and was made in France; the French have always been particularly imaginative about packaging goods, especially confectionery. A china or bisque doll was often used as the finishing touch on a lavishly decorated lid for a box of chocolates, and these, being mementoes, were frequently preserved.

Opposite above

A wax-over-composition doll of about 1880. She is superbly dressed in silk as a lady of fashion, complete with drop earrings. The wig is of mohair, finely braided, rolled and curled in the current fashion, and she has composition arms, and legs with painted boots. Apart from the fading of the painted features, which gives her a rather wan look, this doll is in very fine condition possibly because it has been stored in a constant temperature. Atmospheric changes can sometimes cause cracking in the thin wax with which the head is coated. This doll has withstood the ravages of time very well.

Opposite below

Cuno and Otto Dressel, the firm which made this doll, was founded in Germany in 1700 and is the oldest doll firm for which there are continuous records. Their dolls are usually extremely pretty and this one, with a wax-over-composition head, is no exception. She has the firm's Holz-Masse trademark on her upper leg. Unlike the early wax-over-composition dolls which were painted before being dipped in thin wax, those of the 1880s had the plain composition head dipped into thicker wax before the colouring was applied. If the cheek colouring has faded, a little powder rouge often gives the doll a better appearance.

Dolls of Many Kinds

PAPER DOLLS

Below

Cut-out paper dolls, originally called 'English dolls', have never lost their popularity. When they were first introduced in 1791 they were expensive, but with the invention of a machine for printing them, the price was reduced and they soon became a very popular child's toy. The Victorian ballerina is a cut-out paper doll with a fabric costume. Cotton was attached to the limbs at the back, and when pulled gave this 'Pantin' a realistic dancing movement. 'Pierrette' and 'Pierrot', still uncut after all these years, were printed by Pellerin at Epinal in France; in the quantity and variety of cut-out dolls and toys, he had no equal. The little Victorian paper doll has four changes of outfit.

EARLY RAG DOLLS

Right

Known as a London rag doll, this was a very pretty doll when new. She is not a true rag doll, however, for her face consists of a waxed-muslin mask. The back of the head and body are all in one piece, with leather arms added. A tight-fitting bonnet covers the place where the wax mask is joined to the stuffed head.

This little doll came in a coffin-like wooden box with a religious text dated 1870 entitled 'Little Lizzie's Last Day', which ends with the words 'Heaven is her Home'. As this doll has never been played with, one sadly assumes that some Victorian child never survived to enjoy her toy.

Far right

This sailor boy doll was some Victorian child's loved toy. Eight inches in height, it dates from about 1875. The head is of a material which has been stiffened and then thickly painted. The stuffed body is dressed in a sailor suit with a silver anchor on the collar. The linen hat is stiffened and he carries a tiny yacht only two and a half inches long. This must surely have been a little boy's toy and one wonders if the boy himself eventually went to sea.

GLAZED CHINA-HEADED DOLLS

Left
An unusual boy doll of the type first patented by Motschmann in Germany in 1857. It has a china swivel head on a shoulder plate. The middle part of the body, the upper arms and the upper legs are of cloth. The pelvic section and lower arms and legs are of china (but not jointed as was the Motschman wax-over-composition doll shown on page 18). The head has brown painted hair with brush marks. This doll was probably made about 1865 for there are heels on his shoes. Prior to 1860 all dolls had shoes modelled without heels.

Opposite above
Glazed porcelain dolls are known as 'china heads' to differentiate them from the unglazed porcelain which is known as 'bisque'. This doll has china half-arms and half-legs on a stuffed cotton torso. The contemporary clothes, all in matching fine cotton, date her at about 1865. This style of hair with sausage curls all round was carried on without change right to the 1920s. The quality was less fine as the years went by. These dolls are difficult to date accurately unless one is lucky enough to find one in its original clothes.

Left
This is a reproduction china doll. I have included it to show that these dolls, which are made today, can appear to be genuine Victorian dolls to the inexperienced collector. There is nothing wrong with them provided one buys them knowing that they are modern; unfortunately many are made solely to be passed off as antique. There are, however, some makers of exquisite reproduction dolls in both china and wax who have sufficient pride in their craftsmanship to see that their name is clearly marked on the doll, and many of these will undoubtedly be collectors' items of the future.

Opposite below
These glazed heads, photographed in front of a mirror to show the detail of the hairstyles, are not contemporary with one another. The largest has hair puffed at the sides and then caught in a snood at the nape, and was made about 1865. The smallest is made of pink-tinted porcelain, and is known as a lustre china head. She would have been made about 1840. The head with the gold-painted bow is sometimes known as Empress Eugénie and dates from 1860. These are all unusual heads, the types a collector would hope to find.

EARLY BISQUE DOLLS

Left
This outstanding doll has a bisque head with the bonnet and flower trimming moulded on the head and she is very pretty. She is believed, by the family who owned her, to have been modelled on the young Queen Victoria, and was made about 1840. These bonnet dolls are rare, especially in such fine condition as this, with all the original handsewn clothes: a find like this one will make the true collector feel that all the searching was worthwhile.

Opposite above
These finely dressed dolls were part of the retinue of a wax bride doll. They are rare, for unlike the majority of parian-type dolls, they have inset glass eyes rather than the usual painted eyes. All are of good quality, with well-moulded hairstyles, and they are dressed identically in silk with lavish lace and ribbon trimming. The crinoline, which had been decreasing in size since its maximum width in 1862, was now superseded by the bustle, and these fashionable dolls all show that they have the correct silhouette for the 1870s.

Left
Another doll which was possibly dressed as a tribute to the royal family, who were often photographed in the clothes they wore during their holidays in Scotland. This doll has a pink leather body and arms of bisque. The face has side whiskers painted and then fired into the bisque. This type of doll is often called 'parian' by collectors, which is technically inaccurate: 'parian' is white and these dolls are of tinted bisque. Such dolls with moulded hair were not known before 1870.

Opposite below
This fine doll has a superbly modelled bisque head of the parian type with a very elaborate hairstyle. The painted eyes are highlighted and her cheeks and lips very delicately coloured. She has moulded detail on her shoulder plate with buttons down the front. The cloth body has wooden lower arms and legs and the dress is contemporary, although it does not do justice to her moulded bustline, which makes one think she was not as prized when she was first bought as she would be to any collector today, 100 years later.

UNUSUAL DOLLS

Above
This is a fortune teller doll with a head of glazed china made about 1865. The skirt is composed of folded sheets of pastel-coloured paper. It was the custom at Victorian tea parties to display one of these dolls and then after tea, great excitement was caused by the messages these 'fortunes' gave the readers. All this doll's 'fortunes' are in French. The English translation of one of them is 'Prepare for a trip to the South'. Another is 'Your next meeting will settle the question' and a third, calculated to arouse mixed feelings: 'By the death of one you love you will inherit a fortune'.

Opposite above
A pair of wooden dolls about 1830 which have been dressed in delicately coloured shells. They were probably decorated in France where, along the west coast, there was an abundance of pretty shells easily available. All kinds of materials were used as novelties for dressing dolls. Some have clothes composed of rice grains, and some rice dolls have patterns worked with carraway seeds or very tiny coloured beads. When children had to amuse themselves, they turned to any easily available material. To our eyes now these may seem overdecorated, but the skill and ingenuity even young children displayed fills one with amazement.

Opposite below
A group of pedlar dolls all very different in type. It was a peculiarly British pastime in the early Victorian period to dress a doll as an itinerant pedlar and collect minute articles to display in her basket. Most of these pedlar dolls seem to have been general dealers, but occasionally one finds a doll specializing in a particular commodity, such as fish, bread or baskets. Miniature items for these pedlar trays could be bought in the shops, but the majority of items were handmade, and one of the features of these trays is the small scale of the knitting and the writing on the labels which sometimes gave the licence number of the trader.

UNUSUAL DOLLS

Above
Among novelty dolls, many of which enjoy greater success with adults than children, an interesting type is the two-faced doll. This one, made by Fritz Bartenstein in Germany in 1880 of wax over composition, has one face smiling and the other crying. The hood was removed for the photograph so that both faces could be seen at once, but the hood, covered with a frilly bonnet, is meant to conceal one face at a time. To effect a change of mood, a string in the body of the doll is pulled, the head swivels round and the new expression appears.

Right
Another multi-faced doll, a bisque-headed three-faced one made by Carl Bergner in Sonneberg in 1904. We see the laughing face disappearing and the sleeping face coming to take its place. The third face, behind the hood, is crying. The head is turned by means of the metal knob at the top, which is usually concealed by a bonnet. This doll was later copied in composition but, as with wax two-faced dolls, its popularity was short lived. These character heads are probably more popular now among collectors than they ever were in their own time.

French Dolls

POUPEES MODELES

Below left
An exceptionally beautiful doll with, unfortunately, no marking to help identify her maker. She is dressed in a simple muslin dress with handmade lace trimming, and all her under garments are very finely sewn. She does not appear to have been played with for 100 years, for she still has the original hair ribbon on her immaculate ringlets, and her earrings and necklace with the heart pendant.

Below right
Poupée modèle is the name given to a bisque-headed doll (also often called a French fashion doll). One of the larger fashion-type dolls, this one is 26 inches high. The swivel bisque head is on a shoulder plate which has the impressed F.G. mark. There is some doubt as to who made these dolls; bisque heads with the F.G. mark are usually attributed to Gaultier, and the bodies to Gesland. From a price list for Gesland dolls it would appear that E. Gesland had a factory at 5, Rue Beranger, Paris, with a shop above, and he advertised that the dolls made there were not sold in any other shop in Paris. The Gesland family of dollmakers had initials of A. and E. and F. at various times, which only adds to the confusion.

Opposite above
Dolls like those pictured here parading in an art gallery were the delight of their lucky owners, as new outfits could be purchased for them, and they could always be kept in the height of fashion. *Poupées modèles* were luxury toys, usually with gussetted kid bodies and fine quality bisque heads on a shoulder plate. The doll in the purple and black striped outfit has a most unusual flange-type neck, which allows only movement from side to side, and no forward or backward movement as a swivel head permits. Unless the trademark was impressed, one can only hazard a guess as to who made these dolls, for few of them still carry their maker's label.

Opposite below
This doll and the trunk of clothes were evidently meant for each other, for although they were acquired from totally different sources, the clothes exactly fit the doll. It is interesting to see how dolls like this one were sold; when bought recently this was in its original box, wearing a white muslin shift, blue earrings, blue necklace and hair ribbon to match. In the box with the doll was a white felt hat trimmed with blue, and on the underside of the box lid is written in French: 'Adelina Léonie born October 11 1871 in Paris, rue des Petits Champs'.

FRENCH BÉBÉS

Left
This doll has the most remarkable glass eyes, large and very bulbous. Although it is believed that the first glass eyes for dolls were made in England, most of the eyes for the beautiful bisque dolls of the 19th century were made in either France or Germany. The eyes in this doll must surely be French of the type known as 'paperweight' eyes which have depth, and so bear a startling likeness to real eyes. This doll has the F.G. mark on her head.

Below left
This fashionably dressed doll was originally bought at the Magasin des Enfants, Passage de l'Opéra, Paris, in about 1880. The shop was owned by Marchal and Buffard, who advertised that they only sold exclusive articles. Edouard Marchal was a dollmaker but the shop also sold dolls produced by other famous firms and this one was made by the firm of Jules Steiner. She has fixed eyes, but at this time Steiner was perfecting a sleeping-eyed doll with the mechanism operated by a wire behind the ear. The original dress of this doll is made of lace with ribbon insertion.

Right
These four dolls were made at the factory of Casimir Bru who was famed for the superb quality of his dolls, and they are prized collectors' items today. By the time these dolls were made Casimir Bru had already patented 21 inventions for new types of novelty dolls: dolls which could make a crying sound, a nursing baby which could take milk from a bottle, a two-faced doll, one with a breathing mechanism in its chest, an unbreakable doll made of rubber, and others. Bru also patented many improvements in the articulation of the limbs. The largest of the dolls in the photograph has a bisque head and shoulder plate on a kid body with bisque half-arms; the other three are on jointed wooden bodies. The tiny doll is 'size 1', and she is marked 'Bru' on both the head and the body. Fewer dolls were produced by the Bru factory than by the rival firm of Jumeau, so 'Brus' have a rarity value today which is only surpassed by the elusive 'A.T.' dolls. Because of their desirability, 'Brus' are now being reproduced and sold as 'antique', so one has to buy with care and knowledge.

FRENCH BEBES

Previous pages
This is a 'Bébé Jumeau', made by the most famous and the most prolific of all the French dollmakers. She has a trunk of clothes, not bought from one of the famous shops who sold fashionable outfits, but all lovingly made by some young child, no doubt under the watchful eye of her nanny or mother, for the tiniest stitches have been used and the under-garments have very tiny feather-stitch edging. The trunk, which has a tray and drawer, is packed with waist petticoats, combinations, corsets, drawers, nightgowns and dressing gown, vests and four dresses. The trunk has a label addressed to: The Misses Sara and Judith Francklin, Gonalston Hall, Nottingham.

Top left
This doll is dressed in a uniform of a much earlier period for it was only made in the 1880s. This type of doll with a solid crown is usually referred to as a 'Belton type'. I have never seen a Belton marked doll, and it is possible that dolls

with this different type of head were made by any of the lesser-known dollmakers in Paris. Such dolls have two holes in the crown of the head through which the elastic can pass for stringing the doll. This also facilitates the use of different wigs, for instead of having to glue the wig to the crown one can fix it to the elastic with a hairpin.

Above left
The open mouth with teeth showing, and the fixed eyes, give the date of this Jumeau doll about 1890. In 1896 Jumeau patented a moving eye; after that time most of the firm's dolls were made with 'sleeping eyes'. This was considered a most desirable feature to look for when buying a doll. Today fixed eyes are usually preferred as they are believed, often mistakenly, to be earlier dolls. Jumeau proudly displayed his name on the box lid, on the side of the box, on the doll's head and on her body and shoes, so no one had any doubt at which factory this was made.

Top right
This doll has a label stating that she was

awarded the prize for the 'best dressed doll in all England in 1878'. She is a jointed doll, made by the firm of Rabery & Delphieu in Paris, and dressed exquisitely as a baby. The lace on her dress is all hand-made including the lace insertion. The tucking has stitches which are invisible to the naked eye, which must have been done by an adult especially for the competition, for the doll does not appear to have been played with, but fortunately preserved for us to see and admire.

Right
Advertised as 'l'Universal' this doll, with limbs of hollow wood which established it as the lightest and yet most solid doll made at the time, was bought in Paris in 1892. She has the mark of the Jullien factory on her body and on her head. A luxury doll, she walks, talks and sleeps. When all the French doll companies later got into financial difficulties Jullien was one of the firms which amalgamated with the other major companies to form the 'Société Française de Fabrication de Bébés et Jouets', known usually by the initials S.F.B.J.

FRENCH BÉBÉS

Above
Two attractive toddler dolls made by the
S.F.B.J. company in 1907. The little
girl's head has the mould number 236
and that on the boy is 251. These dolls'
heads could be bought either on a bent-
limb baby body or on the chubby jointed
toddler body. They add variety to any
collection, as one usually gets a
preponderance of the pretty-girl type
dolls. These, with their twinkling eyes,
appear to have character. The S.F.B.J.
range of character heads usually bear one
of the numbers from 203 to 252, and
were made in both white and brown
bisque.

Opposite above
Both these dolls, the one on the left
having a closed mouth and the other an
open mouth with teeth, bear the mark

E.D., which possibly refers to Ernst
Decamps, a junior member of the firm
Roullet and Decamps, who married the
daughter of M. Roullet, the founder of
the firm. Unfortunately, there is no
documented proof that E.D. refers to
him, and during the second half of the
19th century there were several minor
French dollmakers with the initials E.D.,
including Emile Douillet who was a
partner of Emile Jumeau. The dolls'
picnic case is French and it includes the
carafes and the glasses for the wine.

Opposite below left
I have included this doll to show that
if a doll has fixed 'paperweight'
eyes and a closed mouth this does not
necessarily mean she was a Victorian doll
of about 1880. This doll was made by
the company Les Bébés de France which
was only in operation from 1919 to
1921, and used the initials B.F.

She is an interesting doll of fine quality.
Luxury dolls like this, in the lean years
after World War I, may have been out of
the range of the majority of children,
which would account for the short
existence of this firm.

Opposite below right
This doll in her fancy dress costume was
produced by the S.F.B.J. company, and
has one of its rarer mould numbers – 238.
She has the laughing face and sparkling
eyes of character babies, but this mould is
of an older girl. For some reason this
could not have been a popular selling
number although the face is very
attractive and the quality of the bisque is
excellent. It must have been one of the
early models put out when the company
was first formed. Later the quality
deteriorated, and especially after World
War I, the colouring of the bisque
became rather ruddy.

German Dolls

Below left

The corset-fitting room has two unusual occupants – composition jointed dolls with adult figures. Both dolls have heads made by Simon and Halbig, with the mould number 1159; the larger, made for the French market, is of finer quality. Although the dolls' bodies are entirely different, they are both from French factories. The larger has 'La Patricienne' stamped on the hip and was made by E. Daspres in 1907 after he had succeeded Steiner as head of the firm. She was advertised as 'a worldly doll'. The smaller doll's body was made by Jumeau.

Below right

German doll manufacturers made bisque-headed dolls with kid bodies in competition with the later French poupées. Not many of these early heads were marked and these two bear the initials and mould numbers of Simon and Halbig. The firm of Simon and Halbig specialized in making dolls' heads and supplied most of the major companies in France and in Germany. They are fine quality dolls with stationary glass eyes, closed mouths and bisque lower arms. The heads are interesting for they are completely enclosed, but without the holes in the crown for threading the elastic through.

Opposite above

When Germany started to overtake France in the mass production of bisque-headed dolls in the early 1890s, their first dolls were very like the French. This pretty doll made by the firm of Armand Marseille with the mould number 1894 is often mistaken for a French doll. The

bisque is of fine quality and the stationary eyes are of blown glass. Determined to cut production costs so they could sell these dolls more cheaply than the French, the Germans put fine heads like this on poor quality bodies, with shapeless upper legs. Fortunately in the long clothes of the period the legs did not show.

Opposite below

A luncheon party for three. The doll on the left has the mark of Heinrich Handwerck but as he is believed to have used heads from the Simon and Halbig factory all these dolls' heads were probably made there, the other two dolls having the S & H mark on their heads. The one in red, with mould number 1079, is the most frequently found doll from this factory, since one third of the heads made there bear this number, and as it was made for many years, it is very difficult to date. The very pretty doll on the right of the group has one of the rare numbers – 1339.

GERMAN DOLLS

Above left

The most popular doll ever made. She carries the mould number A.M. 390 and most little girls from 1900 to the late 1920s would have had one of these. They were made by the Armand Marseille firm in all sizes up to 40 inches. The earlier ones were of very good quality which does not appear to have been regained after World War I. This doll was bought in the early years of the century and is in very good condition although she has clearly been played with. She has a fully-jointed body, blue sleeping eyes

with real eyelashes and a real hair wig — what more could a child ask for?

Above right

A Red Indian doll made at the Armand Marseille factory. The head is finely modelled in bisque with glass eyes, and the body and limbs are of composition. This is one of a series of dolls made with non-European type heads. Previously, dolls with European features had been coloured and dressed as Indians, Chinese, and Negroes, but the new series was especially modelled and very popular. Such dolls were not like the costume dolls of today, bought as a memento of

a holiday spent in a faraway place, but were bought just as play dolls. The costumes were reasonably accurate for so inexpensive a doll.

Right

Superbly dressed as an Indian gentleman, this doll was made by Armand Marseille. It was probably the toy of a British child who lived in India and had her doll dressed out there. The trousers are gold brocade and the coat and turban are jewel encrusted; they are all lined and lavishly trimmed. The black moustache and hair are painted on, the head being the normal little girl mould number 1894.

GERMAN DOLLS

Above

We now come to the period of the character doll, which has become so popular with collectors today. Kammer and Reinhardt brought out their first character doll, called 'Baby', in 1909. This bears the mould number 100. The large baby doll sitting on the floor is a good example of this type, now popularly known as the 'Kaiser baby'. This doll usually has painted eyes, unlike the doll sitting in the high chair which has sleeping glass eyes and the mould number 116A, which was made later. These heads can be on baby- or toddler-type bodies.

Right

This doll, made by the firm of Simon and Halbig, is very definitely of 1920s vintage: all her clothes are original and from them we can date her; also she has the deeper-coloured bisque with red cheeks and shaded eyelids which were popular in the '20s. Her legs are also made differently from those on earlier dolls, having a short top leg and showing the knee on the longer lower part. They were designed like this to take the short skirt which was then so fashionable. This doll has the mould number 1078 which was used for about 35 years. This mould number and number 1079 are the two most frequently found from this factory.

GERMAN DOLLS

Previous pages
This is another of the Kammer and Reinhardt character dolls. Her mould number is 109 and her name is Elise. These dolls were all modelled on real children, and the child this one represents is Reinhardt's nephew wigged and dressed as a girl. The firm achieved great success in the years immediately preceding World War I and they brought out many different character heads. The mould numbers started at 100 and went as far as 128 but not all these character heads have been traced and documented.

Top left
The doll sitting on the right is another character doll from the firm of Kammer and Reinhardt, brought out in 1909, after the Kaiser baby had been so successful. The mould number is 101. With this wig she is known as 'Marie'; with a shorter wig the name would be 'Peter'. The doll on the left is difficult to identify. It might be from the Kestner factory for that firm did produce some character dolls with painted eyes, and the

mould number, 178, is similar to the Kestner numbers. This doll has a very unusual head, almost completely enclosed at the crown, the small opening having a tiny cardboard disc.

Above left
This is a fine example of the early baby doll made by the firm of Armand Marseille just before World War I. It was first produced with a soft-cloth body but later rounded bent-limb baby bodies of composition were produced for them. Although both types of body were made for a time after Germany regained her markets in the early 1920s, the soft body was eventually superseded by the composition one. Little girls loved these bald-headed dolls which were so like a new baby, and they proved so popular that their production was continued until well into the 1930s. The same mould was still used even then, but for a composition head which did not prove as popular as the earlier bisque heads.

Above right
This doll, with the Kammer and Reinhardt mark on the back of her

celluloid head, has 'flirting' eyes. The head is from a similar mould to the baby head numbered 126. In 1908 the firm had registered a trademark 'The Flirt' for a doll which had eyes which moved from side to side as well as slept; later this new type of eye movement was incorporated in different types of doll including the baby dolls. This doll dates from the 1920s. The body has not been broken in half — it was made in two pieces when a voice box was inserted so that the mechanism would be more accessible, and was sold taped together just like this.

Right
Following the popularity of the Kammer and Reinhardt character dolls, other firms quickly produced their own versions of this quick-selling type of doll. The firm of Gebrüder Heubach had notable success and this attractive doll is from their factory. The painting of the intaglio eyes of these dolls is especially fine, and the quality of the bisque is good, yet these heads are often found on an inferior body, probably to keep the price competitive with all the other German firms making character dolls at the time.

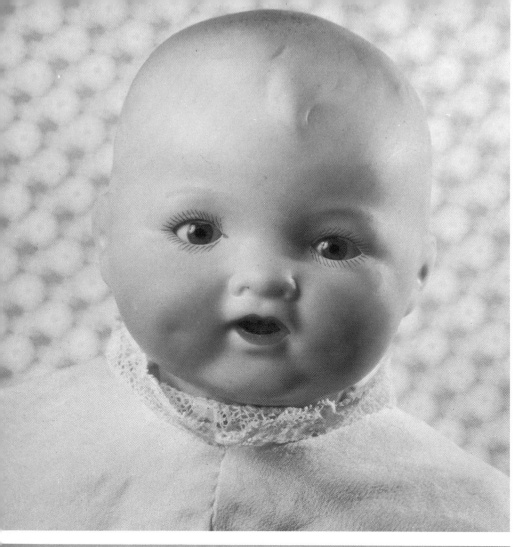

GERMAN DOLLS

Left
'Baby Gloria' is the name impressed on
the back of this attractive baby-type
head. Armand Marseille is believed to be
the maker of the doll, which has a flange-
type neck attached to a cloth body
incorporating a squeak box. It has
sleeping glass eyes, two upper teeth and
dimples. This is one of the many 'named'
dolls which are collected today. Although
baby dolls were popular, all the
manufacturers registered various names
under which to market their dolls, since
they found that a doll with a name was
more appealing to a child.

Opposite above
Two Oriental-type baby dolls, with café-
au-lait-coloured bisque heads, made by
the firm of Armand Marseille. The one
on the right was made about 20 years
earlier than the smaller baby, which bears
the 'Ellar' mark on the back of its neck.
The latter was not made until the mid-
1920s. Those made before World War I
were of finer quality and much heavier in
weight than later ones. English children
were very fond of the Oriental babies but
they usually took off the Eastern-style
shirt in which they were sold and dressed
them in long European baby clothes.

Below left
A small all-bisque doll with roguish eyes
that glance to the side and are known as
'googly' eyes. All the major doll
manufacturers seem to have made dolls
with this type of eye, some in quite large
sizes with enormous eyes, out of all
proportion to the rest of the face. These
are happy looking little dolls and would
have appealed to a young child. In the
United States at this time Rose O'Neill
was having tremendous success with her
'Kewpie' dolls, which had a similar
expression to these 'googly' eyed dolls,
although their eyes were usually painted.

Opposite below
A realistic baby from Kestner at
Waltershausen, another German factory.
This is an appealing baby with glass eyes,
finely modelled head with brush strokes
suggesting hair. It has the mouth often
found on character babies, known to
collectors as an 'open-closed' mouth,
meaning that there is no actual opening
in the bisque but the mouth is moulded
in an open position, sometimes with the
teeth and the tongue also moulded.
Kestner was the only known German
manufacturer who made entire dolls –
heads, bodies, eyes and wigs.

American, English & Mechanical Dolls

AMERICAN DOLLS

Below
This is a 'Chase Stockinet' doll, first manufactured in 1893 and used even today in some American hospitals for instruction in how to care for a baby. The heads of these dolls were made by stretching an elastic fabric called stockinet over a mask, which was then sized and painted with oil-based paint so that it could be washed. The features were hand-painted, and thick rough strokes of paint were brushed on the top of the head to simulate hair. Besides baby- and girl-type dolls, the maker, Martha Chase, also produced characters from *Alice in Wonderland* and from the books of Charles Dickens as well as familiar characters from American children's books.

Right
An all-leather 'Rawhide' doll, of a type rarely seen outside the United States. The head is beautifully modelled – the rawhide would have been first saturated, then pressed into shape and later painted. This doll's head fits into a socket and swivels, and the wrists are jointed. The face is delicately coloured and the blue painted eyes have real hair eyelashes. She is wearing a print dress, and on her real hair wig is a matching mob cap. When I was offered an American 'Rawhide' doll I wondered what it would be like as I had never seen one. I certainly did not anticipate such an attractive doll.

AMERICAN DOLLS

Above

The 'Kewpie' doll is usually thought of as a 1920s doll. Rose O'Neill, an American artist, actually designed them prior to 1912, for it was in that year that they were first manufactured. The early Kewpies were made mostly by European manufacturers, in either bisque or celluloid; but later they were made in all kinds of material. The two illustrated here are of rubber (left) and celluloid (right). Most Kewpies had painted eyes and moulded hair, but some were made with glass eyes and hair wigs. They were made in many positions: sitting, standing, lying and kneeling; and some of the later ones even had jointed bodies.

Opposite above

The Schoenut family were wood carvers in Württemberg. In 1867, one of the sons, Albert, emigrated to America. Though only in his early twenties, he started a factory in Philadelphia to make wooden toys. The first dolls he made were circus clowns, and he perfected a spring-jointed doll which could hold its limbs in any position. After he died in 1912, he was succeeded by his sons, one of whom, Harry E. Schoenut, created the baby doll lying here; its head carries his copyright symbol, a 'C' within a circle. The doll is all of wood, finished with enamel oil paint. The little brown baby in the photograph was made by Eisenmann in Germany, but distributed in the United States.

Opposite below

The Alexander Doll Company was founded in New York City in 1923 by the daughter of a Russian immigrant who had a dolls' hospital there. Madame Alexander has given her name to a range of composition dolls, mostly character dolls from books and films. At the time these dolls were made, they portrayed the most famous babies in the world – the Dionne quintuplets who were born in Canada in 1934. Annette, Emilie, Marie, Yvonne and Cecilie all have their names embroidered on their bibs and they were sold in their bed, as shown here. They were also portrayed later as toddlers and then as little girls. These dolls have now become much-prized collectors' items.

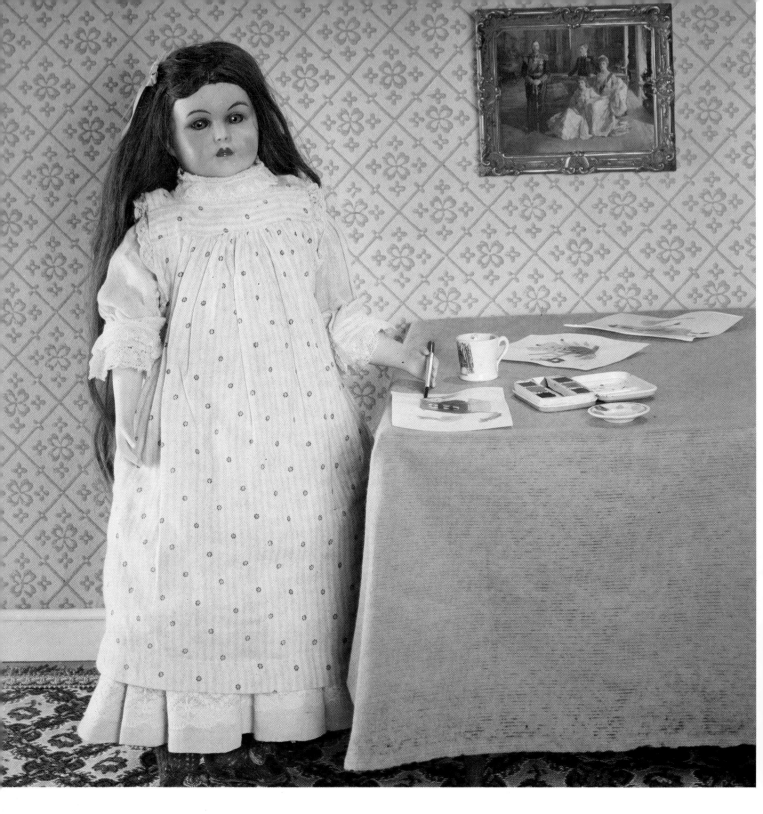

ENGLISH DOLLS

Above

The firm of Goss and Company of Stoke
on Trent is better known today as the
manufacturer of heraldic china, but they
did make dolls, from about 1890. The
quality was not good and did not
compare favourably with that of French
or German dolls, the colouring, especially
of the lips which were very dark red,
being particularly crude. The Goss doll
shown here is one of the prettiest of their
girl dolls. She has fixed blue glass eyes, a
cloth body and bisque lower arms and
legs. Goss also made several baby dolls
with character heads now considered very
desirable by collectors for their rarity.

Opposite above

These English dolls made during World
War I have been carefully preserved for
almost 60 years, beautifully dressed in
the uniform of a St John Ambulance
Brigade nurse. The minute initials
S.J.A.B. can be seen on the epaulettes of
the one in outdoor clothes. The initialled
attaché case and the badges on the sleeve
of her coat and on her cap are realistic
touches, as is the hot water bottle
at the belt of the doll in indoor
uniform.

Opposite below

The shoulder head on the left has the
name 'Tam O'Shanter' incised on the
back, together with the maker's name,
'Hancock'. When the hat is moulded in
one with the head it is known as a
'bonnet head'. The maker, S. Hancock &
Sons, had a porcelain factory at Cauldon,
Staffordshire from 1891; this head was
probably made in the early 1920s. The
modelling of the head is well done, but
the quality of the bisque is poor and it
was not fired after the colouring was
applied, so that now only a vestige of the
red paint is left on the tam o'shanter. The
other head is a German Minerva tin head.

MECHANICAL DOLLS

Above

Two dolls have been included in this section which are not true mechanical dolls but they are both difficult to categorize. This is a toy for a baby, for it is similar to a rattle. The French doll's head is mounted on a squeak box and fitted on to a wooden handle in a way which allows the head and body part to swing from side to side. The wooden hands at one time held bells, and the wooden handle is also a whistle, so this was quite a noisy little toy to distract a baby. Whistles were often incorporated in the handles of musical toys.

Top right

The second doll which is difficult to place in a group of dolls is this one, made by the firm of Bucherer in Switzerland in the early 1920s. This is a metal ball-jointed doll, the neck, shoulders, elbows, wrists, hips, knees and ankles all being jointed. The firm's name is stamped on the tin body and the doll was sold dressed and undressed. These dolls were

made with a variety of moulded composition heads, men's and women's heads, and character heads such as the one shown here. The heads were interchangeable, as the ball joint was attached to the neck and just clipped into the socket.

Above right

A toy consisting of doll figures with movement mounted on a base containing a musical box is often called an 'automaton'. Some were very intricate, with dolls performing many different movements, while others were very simple, like this one. The arms move up and down as the doll sways from side to side in time to the music. The gentle tinkling sound that came from these musical boxes must have had a calming effect on the children in a Victorian nursery.

Opposite above

'Autoperipatetikos' is the name given to this walking doll, first patented in New York July 15 1862, and later in England. The original doll had a papier mâché

head, but later different types of shoulder head were used, including some of the china ones with interesting hair styles. The walking mechanism, which is clockwork, gives a very realistic walking movement, the doll raising and lowering its feet as it moves along. The print behind the doll shows a group of people watching a walking doll, with a poem underneath explaining that it works by 'secret mechanism, obedient to the springs'. The print is dated 1743 — so the Autoperipatetikos cannot be claimed to be the first mechanical walking doll.

Opposite below

When a handle on this French musical-box toy is turned, the legs and arms of the marching boys' band move in time to the tune, and the dolls do appear to be marching and playing their trumpets and beating the drum. The dolls' heads are moulded in papier mâché. All the clothes and the painting on the box are in their original condition, which is remarkable as this toy dates back to the mid-19th century.

Miniature & Modern Dolls

MINIATURE DOLLS

Below

Little-girls who liked to design and sew clothes for their dolls loved the tiny all-bisque dolls dating from the 1880s. This one is French, jointed at the shoulders and hips with a protective reinforcement of kid on the moving surfaces, and with a swivel neck. This doll was sold in its box with its trousseau. The dresses and coats are beautifully styled and trimmed, and the box also includes the various dainty accessories. It is very rare to come across a boxed doll with its original outfit so complete today.

Opposite above

Two French all-bisque dolls, dressed in crocheted wool outfits. Around 1890, women's magazines carried patterns for making dolls' clothes. They were usually crochet patterns, but some were for knitting and sewing, and little dolls were often dressed in pairs as this attractive couple. The crocheted hats were always most stylish. Such little bisque dolls had two types of wig, one with sausage curls which could be dressed as a boy and the other with a long plait of hair. They were usually blonde or light brown in colour.

Opposite below

Only two and a half inches tall, this pair of bisque dolls was made in Germany, about 1890. They have glass eyes and are of fine quality. Miniature dolls like these are often used for dolls' house families; these two, in their original matching outfits, would make a suitable pair of children for a mother doll in a dolls' house.

MINIATURE DOLLS

Previous pages
Two dolls dating from about 1890. The china doll standing in the bath is known as a 'Frozen Charlotte', but in this case 'Frozen Charlie' would be more appropriate as this doll has male characteristics. This is fairly rare as are all male dolls in the West, although Oriental dolls were made in both male and female forms. The doll dressed as a nanny is a dolls' house type of untinted bisque, known as parian. She has a bald head to which is attached a wig of real hair. She would have been sold undressed, so that she could be dressed and wigged as either a man, woman or child occupant for a doll's house.

Above left
Although these dressed dolls appear similar to the previous ones, they are not all-bisque dolls. The heads are made of bisque, possibly at the factory of Simon and Halbig, but the bodies are of composition. This would enable the doll to be sold more cheaply, and these dolls were very popular from about 1890 until

1914. They were sold dressed and undressed, the outfits of the dressed dolls closely following the popular styles of the day. These little glass-eyed German dolls are dressed ready for a drive in a motor car in about 1905.

Above right
It would appear that military uniform was the most attractive form of male attire to a Victorian miss. In literature it was often the dashing military figure who made hearts flutter faster, and if the number of tiny soldier and sailor dolls is anything to go by, the cult was encouraged from a very tender age. This bisque doll in his dashing officer's uniform represents a typically Victorian trend. The firms of Kestner and Simon & Halbig are known to have made miniature dolls, but unless a doll is actually marked it is difficult to attribute it accurately to a manufacturer.

Opposite above
There is endless variety in the types of miniature dolls made. Those illustrated in this book are shown in their original outfits, demonstrating exactly how these

little dolls were sold. The little Negro all-bisque dolls have very colourful costumes, black tightly curled hair and painted eyes. European children adored these dark-skinned dolls, and although some of them must have been sold as tourist dolls, they were made solely as ordinary playthings for the European and American market. These were made with stiff necks which meant that they were cheaper than the swivel-necked dolls.

Opposite below
Room settings were very popular during the latter part of the 19th century. All these dolls have heads made by the firm of Simon and Halbig, which are on composition bodies. The pupils are dressed in black, with white pinafores. On their desks they have exercise books with the tiniest of pencils and also slates. This schoolroom is a simple room setting; sometimes a drawing room setting was designed which gave considerable scope for using one's own furnishing ideas. Many of these room settings were subsequently glazed so that the contents can still be seen exactly as they were arranged so many years ago.

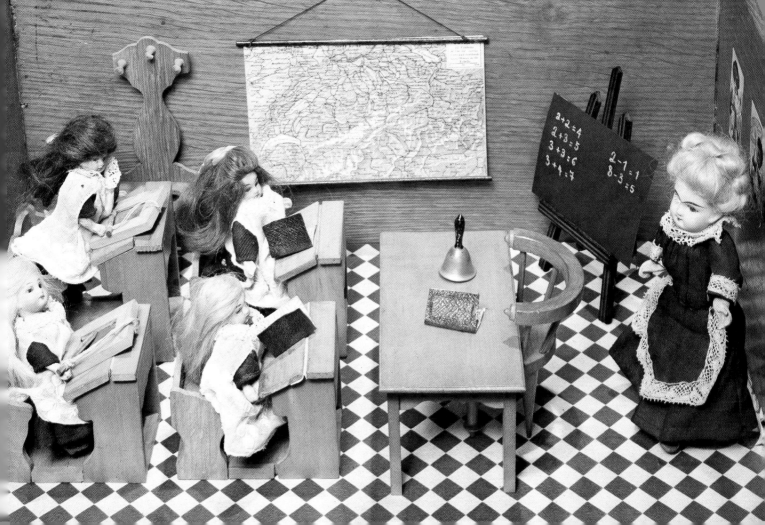

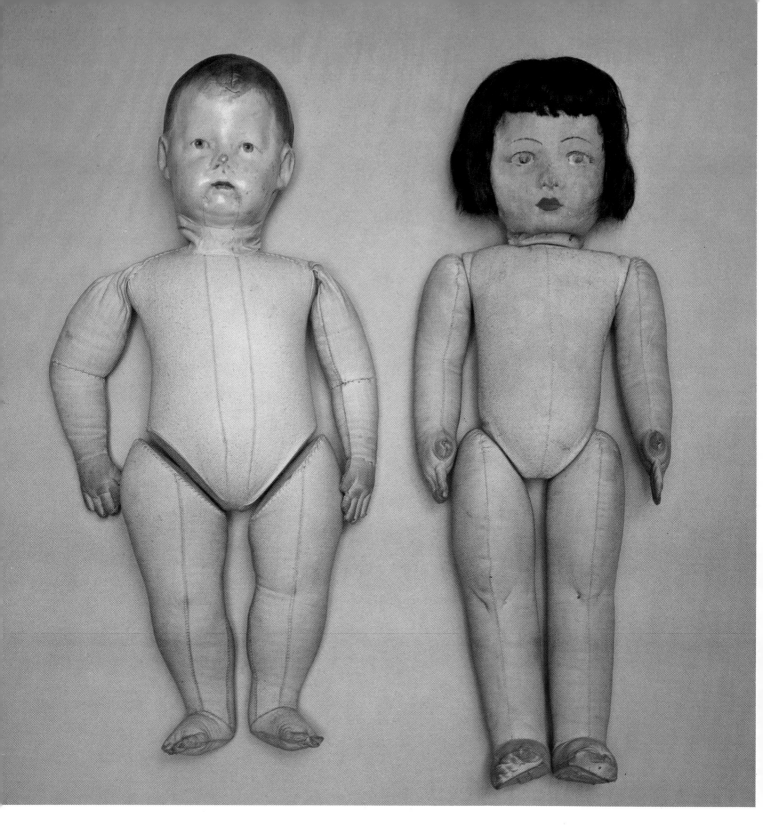

DOLLS SINCE 1930

Above
Cloth dolls are always popular with young children and these two are very well made. The cloth doll on the left was designed by Kathe Kruse and made in the Kruse factory in Germany, which has been making dolls since 1912. The earliest of them were modelled on the artist's children. The cloth doll on the right, with a mohair wig and painted eyes, is from the Chad Valley Company in England. This firm has also made a range of 'royal family' dolls.

Opposite above
Norah Wellings was an artist and dollmaker who designed and made dolls in Shropshire. Many of her dolls were made in velvet, soft to the touch and ideal for a small child. During World War II she designed an R.A.F.. doll with a parachute pack on its back, called 'Harry the Hawk' and part of the proceeds of all sales of this doll went to an R.A.F. charity. All the dolls from this factory carry the maker's name either on the foot or on the clothes. They are all well made and have attractive faces, the ones with glass inset eyes being particularly appealing.

Opposite below
These postwar dolls are made from the material which has revolutionized the doll and toy industry: plastic. The Pedigree doll on the left, purchased in 1952 after the coronation of Queen Elizabeth II, was originally dressed in a peeress's coronation robes. The walking, talking black doll was also made by Pedigree and has rolling and closing eyes. The baby doll dates from 1957 and has the newer type body made of soft plastic, called vinyl. This English doll says 'Mama', drinks from a bottle, cries from ducts by her eyes and wets her nappy.

DOLLS SINCE 1930

Above

Many 'royal' dolls have been made over the years. Queen Anne gave her name to a type of doll, but they were not modelled on Queen Anne herself. Queen Victoria and her children were portrayed in wax and porcelain. In more recent years dolls have been made with a likeness to Princess Elizabeth, Princess Margaret, Princess Alexandra, the Duke of Kent and Prince Michael. One reason for including them in a collection of dolls is that with increasing age they will surely become more valuable. This portrait doll, made of felt, depicts the late King George VI in the uniform of Marshal of the Royal Air Force.

Right

During World War II there was a great shortage of dolls and those made were usually either of all composition or of cloth with a composition face. They were not beautiful dolls but because of their rarity they were very much sought after. The doll on the left must have been pre-war stock for she was made in France in the late 1930s and is one of the type sometimes seen today proudly bearing the label 'Victorian, French'. The air raid shelter setting is very appropriate for all these dolls were bought in London for my own daughter.

WASTE THE FOOD
AND
HELP THE HUN

Acknowledgments

All the dolls in this book belong to the author unless otherwise stated.

Laura Cecil and Angelo Hornak would like to thank the following for their assistance in the preparation of this book:
David Bevan, Felicity Butterwick, Lord and Lady David Cecil, Mirabel Cecil, Jonathan and Phyllida Gili, Richard Heffer, Mrs Joan Knott, Philippa Lewis, Juliet Scott, Miles Thistlethwaite, Joan Wegg-Prosser.

The dolls on page 69 (below) were loaned by Laura Cecil.

The publishers would like to thank Coles of Mortimer Street, London, for their help in supplying wallpapers for many of the illustrations in this book.

MODERN DOLLS

Above

Dolls which are made today must eventually become the collectors' items of the future — who knows which of them will be most prized in 50 years' time? 'Sasha', on the left, was originally made individually in Switzerland, but is now mass-produced in England. On its lap is 'Action Girl', a fully-jointed toy whose counterpart is a doll for boys called 'Action Man'. 'Tracy', the blonde beauty in the centre, is battery-powered; she turns at the waist, bows, and lowers her eyes; she pours out tea and offers biscuits while opening and shutting her eyes. The baby on the right is made of soft vinyl by Pedigree. All these dolls were kindly loaned by Messrs Hamleys of Regent Street, London.